Avalon

Books by Richard Jones

Avalon
Stranger on Earth
The Obscure Hours: Translations
The King of Hearts
The Correct Spelling & Exact Meaning
Apropos of Nothing
The Blessing: New and Selected Poems
The Stone It Lives On
48 Questions
The Abandoned Garden
A Perfect Time
At Last We Enter Paradise
Sonnets
Country of Air
Walk On
Innocent Things
Windows and Walls

Avalon

poems

Richard Jones

Green Linden Press

Green Linden Press
208 Broad Street South
Grinnell, Iowa 50112
www.greenlindenpress.com

Library of Congress Cataloging-in-Publication Data
Names: Jones, Richard, author.
Title: Avalon : poems / Richard Jones.
Description: Grinnell, Iowa : Green Linden Press, 2020
Identifiers: LCCN 2020003726 | ISBN 9780999226353 (paperback)
Subjects: LCGFT: Poetry.
Classification: LCC PS3560.O52475 A96 2020 | DDC 811/.54–dc23
LC record available at https://lccn.loc.gov/2020003726

Cover art: *The Little House,* Pierre-Auguste Renoir
Book design: Madelyn Funk & Christopher Nelson
Text set in Adobe Garamond Pro & Josefin Sans

Green Linden Press is a nonprofit publisher dedicated to fostering
excellent poetry and supporting reforestation with a portion of
proceeds.

Acknowledgments

The American Journal of Poetry: "Contentment," "Light Graces
  My Head with a Halo," "The Proposal"
American Writers Review: "Mercury"
Asheville Poetry Review: "Norfolk, Virginia," "Vase"
Bennington Review: "The Blizzard"
Burnside Review: "Grace"
Cloudbank: "Communion with My 96-Year-Old Mother,"
  "The Island," "Still Life"
Constellations: "The Sedan Chair," "Snakes"
Cultural Weekly: "Blue," "The Desert," "The Distance,"
  "Downsizing," "Dublin," "Khrushchev"
Dialogist: "Ireland"
Escape into Life: "Life above the Sun," "The Mind," "The Owl,"
  "The Secret," "Silence," "Welcome," "Zurich, 1919"
The Hamilton Stone Review: "I Would Sleep on the Roof," "Oil for
  My Lamp," "Quixotic," "Scotland, 1974"
Hiram Poetry Review: "Lilac," "Venice, the Lido"
The Kentucky Review: "The Rope"
MoonPark: "Rain"
New Letters: "The Darkness," "The Shoeshine Box"
Nine Muses Poetry (UK): "Astronomy," "Feeling," "House,"
  "17 Lines"
Pembroke Magazine: "The Tunnel"
The Potomac Review: "The Suitcase"
Presence: "The White Road"
Right Hand Pointing: "Climbing," "Rain in Tokyo"
Sky Island Journal: "Sons"
Under a Warm Green Linden: "Devotion," "Folly," "On Living,"
  "Walking Meditation"
upstreet: "Avalon," "Encounter," "The Great Wall of China,"
  "Morocco," "Purple Potatoes"
West Texas Literary Review: "The Earth"

Contents

On Living   3
The Tunnel   4
Purple Potatoes   6
The Sedan Chair   7
The Rope   8
Rain   10
Life above the Sun   11
The Desert   12
The Suitcase   13
Lilac   14
Silence   16
Still Life   17
Encounter   18
Welcome   20
The Mind   21
The Owl   22
The Shoeshine Box   23
17 Lines   24
Devotion   25
Zurich, 1919   26
Rain in Tokyo   27
The Island   28
Khrushchev   29
Dublin   30
Morocco   32
The Great Wall of China   33
Ireland   34
Feeling   35
Venice, the Lido   36
The Darkness   38

Norfolk, Virginia   40
Scotland, 1974   42
The Blizzard   44
The Distance   46
Vase   48
I Would Sleep on the Roof   50
The Secret   52
The White Road   53
Oil for My Lamp   54
The Proposal   55
Downsizing   56
Blue   57
Light Graces My Head with a Halo   58
Mercury   59
Walking Meditation   60
Folly   61
Climbing   62
House   63
Astronomy   64
The Earth   65
Snakes   66
Contentment   68
Sons   69
Communion with My 96-Year-Old Mother   70
Quixotic   71
Grace   72
Avalon   73

About the Author   75

"Let's call our home *Avalon*,"
Sarah, my daughter, said, "after the island
where apple trees are ever flowering
and kings are healed of their wounds."

Avalon

On Living

First, you must suffer for a thousand years.
Then you must renounce suffering
and dedicate yourself to joy.
Your hands empty, wanting nothing,
you will wander in a forest of silence
and when at last you speak,
your first word will be *yes*
or *grasshopper*.
You will learn to tread on high towering clouds
and to fall—
simple as a stone—
to plummet and tumble straight down.
On your knees with a wire brush you will scrub
the marble floor of the world
and at day's end
wash your cracked hands at a wooden trough.
Though all is waste and desolation,
the moon will rise from desert sands
and cast light and shadow on your old draft horse,
your painted wagon and black tent with its wool blankets.
When the hour's late
and nothing more can be done,
treasure the stillness and peace of the firelight
and sing your song.

The Tunnel

Underneath the house
is a narrow passageway.
I don't know who built it,
only that at any time of day
I can open the secret door
under the table in the kitchen,
descend a dozen steep steps,
and walk with my flashlight
into the grave-like darkness.
The tunnel doesn't go far
and ends in a small chapel,
a den with cold walls of slate.
On a ledge, I keep a lantern.
By its dim light, I offer incense
to sharpen the spirit's senses
and purify a longing for eternity.
Sometimes for my soul's sake
I bring a bucket of water, soap,
and rags to wash away the old
chalk drawings of royal crowns
and the few words and letters
I've scrawled on the jagged walls.
When the stone walls are clean,
I draw white crowns afresh and
sanctify the cave with new words.
The hidden chapel brings me
peace; my thirst is satisfied.
When I extinguish the lantern,
I brave the pitch-dark void—
but only for a moment. Quickly

I return by flashlight to the kitchen
and the table I use as a desk,
finding renewed joy and purpose
in bottles of blue and green ink,
the fountain pen's nib whispering
to the smooth, cream-colored paper.
And when there is nothing to say,
I stroll out to the sunny garden
and enjoy the flowers and birdsong
with my wife and daughter, who
in the clean light of the afternoon
look like two angels in their lawn chairs.

Purple Potatoes

I was enjoying a snack of purple potatoes
when an angel appeared at the table.
"We angels don't covet the ways of men,
neither your sins nor your appetites.
But your potatoes look quite delicious—
and the purple flesh is most beautiful.
Can you tell me what it is to eat
a bowl filled with purple potatoes?"
"It is good," I said. "My body is satisfied
and my soul is nourished by the color."
The angel nodded, considering my words.
I offered to share, to serve the angel a plate,
but the angel raised his hand to say No.
"Purple is the color of mystery and ambiguity,"
I went on, feeling the need to explain further.
"Homer's heroes wore cloaks of Tyrian purple.
Titian and Raphael painted angels in rich
and regal purple robes." (Then I noticed
my angel's robe was the green of his wings.)
"Purple potatoes," the angel said, a little sadly,
before disappearing back into the light.
"Yes," I said loudly to the air, looking around
and wagging my fork, "but still they are just
potatoes." And when the angel did not return,
I finished my meal, enjoying each purple bite
as I scraped and polished the white plate clean.

The Sedan Chair

Should I find myself one day
being carried in a sedan chair
up a mountain's narrow lanes,
I would ask my bearers to stop
when we were nearly there.
In my silk robe, I would emerge
from the floating box and walk,
leaning on my cane for strength.
I'd mount the steep stone steps,
climbing to the town's ramparts.
Atop the wall, I'd take in the view—
green hills below, the valley's blue
smoke, the fields of sunflowers.
I'd consider my frail condition.
If some elegant ladies appeared,
I would not speak to them a word.
I'd let their lovely parade pass by,
my timidity intact and unharmed.
When evening fell on the ancient wall,
a purple sky would inspire raptures
and I would linger in the twilight
beneath the razor cut of the moon.
Then my bearers would lift their poles
and carry me home in the dark,
a linkboy's torch leading the way.
On the road down, behind my curtains,
I would lean and drowse on a pillow
and the sedan would jostle and sway
under the weight of all my dreams.

The Rope

I suppose I was like a drowning man holding on to a rope
thrown from the side of a ship,
though there was no ship,
only vast ocean
and a rope undulating on the waves.
Treading water, I pondered
what it might have looked like had I been saved
by a big white boat
and pictured myself standing on the open deck,
a brown blanket over my shivering shoulders
as I thanked the sailors and the captain,
shaking everyone's hand so gratefully.
I was never pulled to safety
and after a while the ship in my mind sailed on.
But for some reason I could never let go of the rope.
In the middle of the ocean,
the rope became everything to me.
I learned to use the rope
to perform all sorts of marvelous feats.
I could lasso dolphins and sharks
and ride them bareback over the waves
or hang the rope from the crook of a crescent moon
and climb up to the stars.
Eventually it occurred to me to throw the rope
in case someone else needed rescue.
I felt a tug and began to pull.
To better my footing, I swam to a deserted island,
where I tied the rope around a tall palm tree,
planted my foot in the sand,
and then kept pulling until I pulled my wife ashore,

followed by my two sons,
and then my daughter.
My wife wanted to dry her wet clothes in the sun,
so we used the rope for a clothesline,
then as a ladder to climb palms
to pick bananas and coconuts for our hungry children.
At night, when the stars appeared
and the firmament shone over the vastness of the ocean,
the five of us sat around a small fire,
which my boys started with a bow drill
they made from driftwood
and a piece of our rope.
I enjoyed watching them patiently
spinning the bow drill until there was smoke
and a tiny ember they could blow into a flame.
It is a good home the rope has provided.
Tied between two trees, it now
supports a roof of palm branches and leaves,
a fine shelter for my family.

Rain

Rain falls on the tin roof like buckshot,
teaching me something about peace.
It's late April and the rain is a prophecy
about a rich harvest of wheat, grapes,
and olives from an ancient orchard.
I want the rain to tease open the seed
of my heart, to nourish the little flowers
of the mind so they'll blossom and grow,
but nothing is happening. The house is still.
I'm just sitting here in my old armchair,
a book in my lap, my eyes closed, listening.
I am the same bootless man I was before.
So I go outside and the hard rain soaks me,
soaks me and blesses me down to the bone.

Life above the Sun

I had allowed life on earth
to become meaningless
and filled with despair.
So I climbed a tall ladder
and lived above the sun.
My house up there was in
shambles—long-neglected
and in need of much repair.
It felt good to fix the roof,
replace broken windows,
and tear out rotted boards
so the front porch once again
could become a place of rest.
I put dinner on the old stove
and sat in a wooden rocker,
watching afternoon light
sprawl across the meadow,
the blue hills in the distance
a revelation that everything
is of consequence, everything
I do carries great weight.
I'd pruned the wild orchard
and as the night grew cool,
I built a fire of apple wood.
Then I set myself to the task
of stitching my mind together,
that dirty wool blanket—
moth-eaten and full of holes.

The Desert

I didn't know what to make of the waterless riverbed—
the orange sand fine as dust, the broken, scattered rocks.
I followed the path that cut through the arid landscape,
a wide, dry rivulet that curved and pushed forward
through a craggy ravine. I felt like some lost prophet
walking an elegant long brushstroke made by the sky.
Far as my eye could see, the land was barren and lifeless.
I'd not find another living person for a hundred miles.
The sun bright as fire, the day hot, I tried to imagine
the spring river flowing all around me, snowmelt
or sudden storm flood, the water up to my waist,
the current sometimes gentle, sometimes fast,
but always insistent, the water whispering, "Hurry—
we've somewhere to go and we must go there now."

The Suitcase

When I was five I told myself:
if you're going to go to sleep
you'd better pack a suitcase
because there's no promise
the world will be here
when you get back.
Your father will be gone—
he'll fly away like a bird.
And your mother
will be in a distant hospital,
dying, or dead,
and you will never see her
or your father ever again.
The house you live in
and the room you love
will vanish like any dream
and you will find yourself
lost at sea, shipwrecked,
marooned on some green island.
But at least you will have your belongings,
all carefully packed in your suitcase—
your big blue bunny
and tin cup,
your cowboy hat and six-shooters.

Lilac

Yesterday I drove to the garden store
and purchased a lilac, which is now sitting
in front of me in its rectangular black pot.
I take time, pondering where to plant it.
I already have a hedge of full-grown lilacs—
the sweet scent of the mauve blossoms
floats through my open windows in May.
The word for that warm scented breeze
after a long dull winter is *intoxicating*.
How, I ask, could I be blue when I read
the plastic planting guide, which says
I am the owner of a *Syringa vulgaris*,
which is a fancy way of saying I have
a common lilac. Thus *vulgaris*—
the Latin word means "common"—
and *Syringa* because the stems are hollow
like syringes, which reminds me again
of intoxication and addiction, the way
I'm addicted to lilacs—always have been.
The lilac is one of the bushes I remember
from childhood, and the holy perfume
of a cluster of blossoms carries me home
to a country of wax-green ligustrum hedges
and lavishly flowering honeysuckle bushes.
And I've long known the meaning of lilac
in the poetic language of flowers—love,
innocence, tranquillity, passion, and purity.
How can I be sad, sitting here with my lilac,
when to my delight I see my planting guide
is presented in both English and French?

"Planting Guide" *and* "Guide de plantation."
Tell me, how could I be anything but happy,
walking the yard with garden gloves and shovel,
asking my little lilac where it would like to live?

Silence

Some nights I rest in silence.
The lamps on the bed tables
are quiet, and the lightbulbs
sleep in their copper sockets.
The windows let in silence,
just as they welcome the light
during the day. The darkness
holds its breath; even the moon
holds her peace in the sky.
Some nights I wake for a time
and like David in the psalms
I must tell my soul to wait
and not fret, to let silence
do its work. And some days
I'll see a friend on the street.
We'll chat about this and that
and occasionally I am led
to ask, "How is your soul?"
And sometimes friends
won't know what to say
and will just gaze at me,
bewildered and speechless.
But other times I'm blessed
to go with friends and eat
straight from heaven's table,
where we speak sublimely
about the most mundane things.

Still Life

I keep returning to the unfinished painting
dry on the easel, a still life
of yellow apples and a blue pitcher.
In the quiet of my sunny room
I'm free to walk around,
to observe the canvas from near and far
in differing aspects of light.
I close my eyes for a time,
trying to clear my vision.
I stand to the left, the "gospel side,"
as the hour passes and the room grows dim.
In the flickering light of candles,
the painting grows more mysterious than ever,
and I more shadowed and unseeing.
Many days I work like this,
never once mixing paints, never lifting a brush.

Encounter

The eighth blackbird landed
before me on the iron table
under the big red umbrella.
The wings quivered, stilled,
then folded slowly, elegantly.
Yellow rings circled the eyes,
which were two black pearls.
The seven others perched
on the fence in the evening
garden, keeping their counsel
as dusk fell. A glass of wine
turned purple in the last light.
Then the eighth blackbird spoke—
not words, but in a lingua franca
I understood easily, like poetry.
The blackbird told me last winter
it nested in snowy mountains
and had been a friend to eagles.
I said last winter I visited Paris.
Hopping a bit closer, the blackbird
apologized if his early-dawn song
had bothered me. I said no, no,
I was grateful to wake to music,
though I found the song sad.
He told me he had lost his mate
and he was mourning life's brevity,
adding that after every rainstorm
he still sings songs to the fresh air.
Then he asked how I could stand it—
not having wings. It's a miracle

you survive, he said, sitting on your deck
with purple wine in the twilight.
His eyes flashed; his gaze fixed me.
Flying is quicker than human thought,
he said, as if I should know this truth.
I said I had no reply to such a mystery
and waited, anticipating a revelation,
but the bird simply wished me well
and took off, lifting away so suddenly
I started and could not breathe again
until long after the pearl-eyed blackbird
had vanished into the sun's last light
beyond the weeping willow I planted.

Welcome

Down the street from our lane,
a 100-acre working farm has cows
and chickens and a windmill,
a white wooden outhouse with
a crescent-moon window in the door,
tractors and plows, a field of corn
and of alfalfa, a watering trough,
and tall trees with picnic tables.
A red barn piled high with hay
is home to cats that sleep in the loft.
My daughter and I walk to the farm
to hand-feed the lambs; Sarah marvels
at the pigs' adorable curly tails.
If the two big draft horses see us,
they saunter over to the gray fence
hoping for carrots or apples.
Sometimes, large flocks of wild geese
float in Vs overhead and then land
on the fenced meadow's grass hill,
folding their wings and crying out
to my kindhearted daughter, who
welcomes all the geese like family
after their long migration home.

The Mind

*The mind is an ancient
and famous capital*
   —Delmore Schwartz

All down the steps of these long decades
I have enjoyed living inside my mind,
an ancient capital, ruined and eternal,

as great a city as London or Rome,
with pleasant tree-shaded boulevards
and alleys and narrow passageways.

My mind is like a king's walled palace
or a mansion of many rooms with views
of a terraced countryside, river, and sky.

My mind is shelter and sanctuary, a secret
treasure house, a cathedral, a high tower.
It's a forsaken shack found in tall woods
or a cold attic room with a single candle.

At sea on a painted warship, my mind—
bound for distant shores. From a cramped cabin
I send word of my adventures and trials
on a tiny scroll attached to the leg of a pigeon.

The Owl

Although we all fear death,
we're still curious to know
what's on the other side—
black fire? Nothingness?
Streets of gold and light?
I lie awake all night
just thinking about it,
while outside in the tree
the owl's eyes are intent
on the shadows, waiting
for something small to move.

The Shoeshine Box

My father passed it down,
the wooden shoeshine box
with the footstep on top.
I ask my grown son to sit
and allow me the honor
of polishing his boots.
He rests a foot on the step
as I kneel. We say nothing
as I dip my cloth in the wax
and start with the sides,
rubbing the heel and top,
the hard-to-get welt,
taking extra time to blacken
the sole's edge, to polish the scars
and scratches. When all is
tuned up, as my father would say,
I sweep the brush back and forth,
the bristles making shushed music,
the redeemed shoe shining.
"When you're gone," my son asks,
"can I have the wooden box?"
Then he rises and strides forth
as my younger son takes a seat
and my daughter in the doorway
tells me she would be next.

17 Lines

In Chicago for five hundred dollars
you can buy 17 lines in the *Tribune*
to publish your child's obituary,
but many families of the dead
haven't got that kind of money
or the cash they will need to buy
a suit for the son in the casket,
or the money it takes to buy lunch
after the service for all the mourners
to sit together at a table for an hour
and remember, weep, and celebrate
the joy the child gave his bereaved
mother, who bent over the casket
to straighten the blue tie, the mother
who held him in her arms the night
before he stepped out of the house
into the street and was shot in the chest.

Devotion

"Poetry not rest" is trouble's answer,
rising before the sun, setting out
in a gray light to the dull grumble
of thunder to balance the words
bottle or *old wooden chair* or *bluebird*
on a line's life-or-death tightrope,
struggling to add color to the canvas,
purple or burnt umber, transcribing
seven violins crying in the willows,
or simply cutting a stem of rosemary,
the deep smell of earth for inspiration,
the earth and the grave, never resting,
working from sheer will and memory,
working with quill and ink if need be,
knowing trouble and rest won't last,
that no one has the cure for this life
though we honor the day with words,
name the plow and extol the hammer,
knowing that even the poorest poet,
if a poet, is at a desk in a corner
of eternity, already long dead,
laboring to transform *death* to *praise*,
never wearying, never once losing faith.

Zurich, 1919

When I finally came to from my nap,
I thought of Tristan Tzara, the father
of Dada. Had Tzara wished to write
a love letter or send a token of affection
from Zurich, what might he have done?
Perhaps he'd realize the truth: love is
greater than one man and one woman.
I picture him sending a stuffed spotted owl
or an elegant peacock, the plumage alone
greater than anything a poet might say.
Maybe he'd have sent an exquisite corpse
composed with his friends—André Breton,
Louis Aragon, Paul Éluard, and Max Ernst.
Or maybe he'd wrap an empty wine crate
and call it *Handkerchief of Clouds.*
I rolled over in bed, head on pillow, eyes open.
I imagined Tzara donning his monocle
and sending one of the new gramophones
so recently conceived and invented—
the black record spinning, the music flowing
out of a lovely horn made of polished brass
or sculpted mahogany painted with roses.
After all, wasn't it young, monocled Tzara
who extolled spontaneous poetry? Who said,
"I love you because you are simple and you dream"?
Or could I be misremembering? It's a long time
since I read Tristan Tzara. And have I ever—
sitting up and rubbing sleepy eyes—listened
to music flowing like balmy summer breezes
out of the flower-shaped horn of a gramophone?

Rain in Tokyo

After my day wandering the park,
clouds came and I hurried home,
but the smiling Buddha sat all night
in the chill dark and pouring rain.

The Island

He lay in bed in the bright room. He grew still.
He had colored the ceiling a luminous purple
with phosphorescent paints. The high ceiling
a private dream, he reached out, switched off
the bedside lamp, then turned on a black light.
Glued to the ceiling, a blue painting of the sea
sketched with bold and vibrant fluorescent inks
was transmuted in the semidark into a living ocean,
and he became something other than himself,
adrift on the currents beneath sunsparkled waves.
Light shone all around, rays falling like arrows
to touch smooth sand, reefs, and bright coral.
He'd drawn many different kinds of friendly fish—
butterfly fish, angelfish, Moorish idols, damselfish—
all turning toward him in a deft rainbow of color.
When he closed his eyes and let all thought go,
he could feel the fish swim right through him.
Sinking into sleep, his dream a sweet drowning,
he felt certain he was only a few yards off the coast
of a beautiful virgin beach with pure, white sand—
that he was only a moment away from paradise.

Khrushchev

I liked the way Nikita Khrushchev
banged his brown shoe on the table
until he got the world's attention.
Khrushchev reminded me of Picasso,
who outwitted everyone with a bull
made of a bicycle seat and handlebars.
Picasso's obsession with the Minotaur
makes me think of Homer and Ovid
and the painting of Sisyphus by Titian
that hangs in the Prado in Madrid.
The rock given to Sisyphus was meant
as a curse and a punishment, and Titian
captures the hellish darkness and struggle.
But the rock was a gift from the gods,
so doesn't that make it wonderful?
I refuse to believe it is a punishment
to push the heavy rock up the hill.
Every morning I wake, I feel lucky,
and thank the gods for the big gray rock
waiting by my bed. How good it is
to have a rock to set one's heart to
and a mountain I call my very own!

Dublin

"Let's go for a dander,"
my Irish friend said,
so we walked along the Liffey,
then turned to have a drink
at Ryan's with its famous clock,
engraved mirrors, and snug-rooms.
Ryan's is the Victorian bar where
Patrick Kavanagh once held court
and Ludwig Wittgenstein rented
and lived in an upstairs room.
We paused a moment in silence
to contemplate that and drink.
The two of us agreed that in this life
the worst thing that could happen
would be to find our pint gone
flat and tepid. "Lead with a verb,"
my friend advised. "Nothing lasts."
Irish tends to disregard indefinite
articles, using only the definite.
"I'm going to see the mother,"
I told my friend. "She's 96," I said,
"and has no bell on her bike."
My friend wore a yellow blazer.
I sported new black tennis shoes
with fire-red stripes down the heels.
When we got back to our walk,
twilight was falling. Neither of us
could decide exactly what color
to call the sky, but we embraced
the mystic, the mysterious, and the limits

of language. We shook hands
and agreed we'd meet again to find
more things we could not name
and evening skies we had no words for,
knowing that if we walked long enough
and far enough, we could trust the words
to find us.

Morocco

A Swedish girl my age spoke perfect English
and led me through the impossible labyrinth
of the casbah's narrow alleyways, where
she'd barter in French for spices or silk.
Generous and kind, she'd buy live chickens
and wooden cases of bottled Coke carted
on donkeys through the passageways—
sweet and needful things she would give
to the children who followed us each day.
At her posh hotel, we'd rest on the terrace
in blue shade sipping mint tea with sugar.
As the call to prayer drifted over the rooftops
and believers knelt in evening's golden light,
we'd talk about our homes—little, sacred things
we'd remember, odd memories and musings.
We were so young, like a brother and sister.
She invited me to her room; I slept on the floor.
Strange music drifted in though the window
while haunted, alien cries rose from the streets.
As I slipped off to sleep, she told me a story
about the day she left her home and family—
the white ferry, her mother waving a scarf
from the pier, the city she loved disappearing,
the churning sea and flowing sky, her new life
composing itself in a thousand shades of blue.

The Great Wall of China

Walking the long wall's ramparts and battlements,
I stopped in one of the signal towers where,
to my surprise, there was a humble refreshment stand.
A boy—I'm guessing he was twelve or thirteen—
sold me a Coke from an icebox. I gave him a bill
and refused the change, signaling that I wished
only to linger a moment in the quiet tower.
After a few minutes of silence, the boy invited me
with a wave of his hand to climb ancient stairs
to the high lookout. As I regarded the green hills
rolling away for a thousand miles, I imagined
the joy of looking deep into night skies
and seeing only pure darkness rich with stars.
Then I saw the solitary straw mat
on which the boy slept, his few possessions
contained in a canvas bag in the corner,
the forlorn distances of summer afternoons.
On the stone floor there was a water bottle,
a folded brown wool blanket, a bowl,
and a wooden box, closed and mysterious.
Taped to the wall's bricks, a weatherworn
photograph of a young woman in a white blouse.
As high clouds passed above, I turned to go,
but stopped when the boy pointed to the photo,
tapped his heart, and in English told me,
"This is my mother."

Ireland

In Ireland my daughter walked the cliffs
or climbed down rock ravines to the sea.
The frenzied waves crashed and thundered,
drowning out her father's voice calling her.

It was the same on the windblown Burren.
She wandered far off, leaping the clints—
those smooth limestone glacial pavements—
to search the grikes for flowers to press

in her field book: Irish eyebright, burnett rose,
wood sage, mountain avens, oxeye daisy,
orchid and fuchsia, harebell and gentian.
My heart told me *let her walk free*

as I waited by the lonely dolmen tomb
that is thousands and thousands of years old.

Feeling

I carry my blighted rosemary bush outside
to rinse and bathe her with a mixture
of milk and water before I cut her long stems.

In the big yard next door, three gardeners
(whose counsel I have often sought)
plant annuals—a bed of red and white impatiens.

I set aside my dripping rosemary to call out,
"Bendices el jardín con significado espiritual."
You bless the garden with spiritual meaning.

The wise gardeners nod. They also believe
life is about *la música, lágrimas, y alegría.*
They say, *"Hoy es un buen día."* I salute them,

then lift my face to the sun to feel its heat,
strong and absolute. Hand on my chest,
I take a moment to feel my heart beating.

Venice, the Lido

I take my place on the sandy beach,
dropping onto a wooden chaise longue
under a yellow-and-blue umbrella.
In the shade I take off my straw hat,
my long white robe. I look cross-eyed
at my upturned nose to appreciate
the cool, arctic-white zinc oxide,
then apply handfuls of lotion
to my shoulders and plump belly.
I look like an Italian banker
on holiday, a man who knows
not only how to eat and eat well
but also how delicious it is
to lie on a warm chaise and rest.
It's been so long since I've seen the sun,
my skin is wan and ghostly. The locals
blink and gape, never having seen skin
so pale, or a man like a white whale
in red swim trunks and sunglasses.
The beautifully fit and tanned locals
must wonder where I come from:
Geneva, or Bern, or Mont Blanc.
Ah, I sigh, *the white mountain.*
The Adriatic bright, the Italian sky
an unrolled bolt of soft, blue silk—
I let my eyes close slowly and dream
of ascending Mont Blanc in winter,
climbing ropes wrapped in loops
around young, muscled shoulders,
blue carabiners clipped to a sling,

my body hidden beneath insulated pants,
hard shell jacket, and wool balaclava.
The valley disappears in an ocean of mist
as I climb by inches—gripping edges
of rocks with my fingertips, balancing
on small ledges and outcrops of crystal.
The high peaks echo when I hammer
pitons into impossibly tiny cracks of rock,
and only the sun and a few lofty clouds
cheer me on as I dangle from the mountain
at the end of a rope, twirling with my ice ax.

The Darkness

That spring began with a catastrophe—
a baseball with the speed and force
of a cannonball struck me in the left eye.
My mother, called to the hospital,
saw the ruined face, her unconscious boy,
the blood-soaked T-shirt and jeans,
and believing I had been killed, fainted.
After the surgery, my father was told
there was a good chance I would lose
all sight in the eye. I lay in bed,
fed with straws and sleeping
fitfully, my face half-wrapped
in gauze and bandages. Blind dreams
would spin my body on the mattress,
tangled and trapped in the white sheets,
until I had turned around, my head
at the foot of the bed. Each day,
an orderly would lift me in his arms.
To an eleven-year-old boy,
it was like flying or being raptured
while a chatty nurse changed the linens.
Then the orderly would gently
position me so that I rested properly
on the bed, my body the hand of a clock
at midnight or noon, each hour the same.
Three weeks later, the family gathered
as the doctors unwrapped the bandages.
A pair of skilled hands lifted the gauze
in slow, careful circles from my eyes.
It must have been like a scene in a movie—

everyone held their breath and asked
if I could see. I beheld a blue-yellow haze
and then figures, "like trees walking,"
as the blind man said in Mark's Gospel.
I recall that for a moment I did not speak.
A part of me, though young and untested,
knew something had been exchanged,
something purchased. The gift was mine.
My mother took my hand; my father wept.
The light was too much. I closed my eyes
and said to the listening darkness,
Do not be afraid. I see clearly.

Norfolk, Virginia

Because I was little and limber and skinny,
my father asked me to wriggle under the house
and enter that cramped place called "the crawl space."
A tiny green door behind the furnace opened
and I slithered snake-like on my stomach,
breathing the dust, the fine ash in my mouth.

I don't remember what the task was,
but I had a flashlight to show the way,
a thin beam that pierced a darkness
that held nothing at all that I could see.
It seemed to me I had gone down to Sheol
and found no one—no shades, no lost souls.

My father called my name and instructions
I couldn't hear, words I wish to know now,
believing he was saying something more
than just how to get through a crawl space.
He was telling me how to walk a sunny street
or look into a night sky filled with a thousand stars.
But I was far beneath the old Victorian,
and his faint voice was lost in the eerie emptiness.

I remember extinguishing the flashlight,
rolling over on my back, and imagining
the sweet world of the house above me—
the sheer white curtains at the windows,
the two white columns in the broad foyer,
my mother dusting the crystal chandelier
with a long-handled wand of ostrich feathers.

And high upstairs in her room, my older sister,
standing at her easel with palette and brush,
silently contemplating a blue ceramic pitcher
she had placed on a round table beside a peach.

Scotland, 1974

The morning of my twenty-first birthday,
I left Edinburgh and hitchhiked north
on the A9 in the rain. I caught a ride
with a lorry. The young, bearded driver
educated me on the virtues of whiskey
and I was mesmerized by the uncanny
way his musical voice kept perfect time
with the metronome of the wiper blades.
The road narrowed. The land became
wild, mountainous, desolate, beautiful.
The lorry dropped me in the Highlands
in a remote place I couldn't find on the map.

I'd ventured northwest in search of clans—
McEachins, Morrisons, northern Watsons—
my mother's people, the ancient families
with tartan colors and heraldic flags,
though I had no idea where to look
and no set plan to discover them. Perhaps
I just wanted to walk their mountains,
or lie awhile in the ever-changing sun
by a windswept lake, or find myself blessed
with the good fortune to spy a rare sprig
of white heather to slip in my notebook.

After the lorry fled into the mountains,
I realized I didn't know where to go next.
The drizzle turned into a downpour.
I pulled on my poncho, crossed a bridge,
and walked on ahead to the next curve,
mountains rising to the west, a small glen
to my right falling into dark pinewoods.

Hiking boots soaked, rain in my eyes,
I stopped and stood still in that deluge
and reckoned the difference between
where I was and where I was going—
a young man with no name and no home
yet with sense enough to see my only road
was not on the map, and I'd push on alone.

The Blizzard

The B and B in Indianapolis was charming.
I didn't want to leave. I liked the desk
in the parlor, and the good coffee recalled
quiet days in Rome. I stayed upstairs—
a sitting room, a rocker, a comforter.
On Sunday I was the only guest, the others
having left to beat the coming storm.
I could call and cancel my week, I thought,
as I had yet another coffee and opened
my notebook to write an hour longer.
When I finally got on the road,
the first flakes were tumbling down,
and I reprimanded myself for lingering,
for giving in to the frazzled wish
that a cozy room might calm my nerves.
On the highway, snow swirled and raged
and my fantasy came back to rebuke me.
The blizzard had been predicted for days;
the innkeeper had warned me repeatedly.
It wasn't long before the road disappeared
under a white blanket. I couldn't see
any other cars, and suddenly
there were no tracks to follow, no lines—
just the unwritten page before me.
Making my way home like a pilgrim,
I crawled down the road to classical music,
something Romantic, then something
Baroque. Going slow, then slower still,
cellos and oboes my only companions,
I suffered a renaissance of mind.

Then a blessing came from the fields
or the sky—it was all the same now—
and I gave myself over to the blizzard,
driving unhurriedly, listening to Vivaldi,
one hand on the wheel, relaxed, calm,
looking ahead and seeing nothing at all.

The Distance

I was a thousand miles away
in church that Sunday morning
when my mother had a seizure
and collapsed, a thousand
miles away when my sister
put a pillow on the floor
under my mother's head,
a thousand miles away when
the ambulance slowly drove
the narrow, twisting lane and
my mother was lifted and taken
to the hospital. The doctors
performed all the usual tests
and procedures; my mother lay
quietly on a gurney and waited
with my sister for the results.

The call came midday as I sat
by a sunny window in my study,
the light warm on my shoulder.
I talked to God, even though
God was a thousand miles away.
I asked Him what He was doing.
I was curious and wanted to know.
I knew His hand was on my mother,
and He was guiding the hands
of all the nurses and doctors,
and He was in my sister's hand
holding my mother's hand tight.
But I wanted to know what

He was *doing*. Did He offer comfort
I could not imagine, or was His eye
on the eternal things that matter most,
the true things that will last forever?
I found it very hard to see either—
the present moment counted
by jagged blips on a heart monitor
or the life that flows in timeless eternity.
I was a thousand miles away from seeing,
alone in my study, a warm light falling
through the white blinds on my shoulders,
staring into the air, thinking about the distance.

Vase

When the storm came I sat by the window
and opened the red box I'd bought in China,
a box with a scene inlaid in silver stones
of a man contemplating a quiet lake,
peaceful sky and unmovable mountains.
In the box I've saved the pretty tickets
to the National Museum in Beijing,
the Mercy and Kindness Buddhist Temple
in Xi'an, the Yu Garden in Shanghai;
snapshots of monks at an outdoor market
where I bought a jade necklace for my wife;
and a stone I guiltily pocketed at the Great Wall.
I have a postcard of the Terracotta Warriors
buried with the emperor, massed and ready
to protect him in the afterlife from unseen forces.
Around the house, the storm ranted like a madman.
Fierce winds howled in the chimney, the old
windows rattled, lightning flashed, lit the room,
and thunder shook the table. I grew quiet
as the sky rumbled and the house trembled.
Through the window I saw a roof shingle
had torn free and was flying like an omen.
On the lawn I counted many broken branches.
It's said the Lord is a gardener who prunes
dead branches He throws in the fire.
Reflecting, I saw I'd been pruned so hard
so many times, there's almost nothing left of me.
But I still have my red box with its tranquil
silver scene of the man by the still water.
I have my old Chinese coins shaped like keys,

a piece of blue ribbon, and a thank-you note
from a friend I took for tea when word
came from America her grandmother had died.
Her family insisted she stay on in China,
complete the tour and see everything there was to see—
the blue-and-white Ming vase hundreds of years old
yet seemingly untouched by time, as if the potter
had shaped and fired the vase only yesterday,
so beautiful I held my friend's hand as she wept.

I Would Sleep on the Roof

I would sleep on the roof
but the pitch is too steep.
I'd build a booth in a tree
and live there for a season,
eating meals and studying
scripture by candlelight,
but storms took my maples
and the spruce trees are dying.
So once again I set up a tent
and fill it with all the things
I need: books, wine, pens,
lantern, blankets, and pillow.
I sit through the evening
in a half lotus, my old legs
aching a little, but happy,
and listen to a lively wind
flowing from house to house.
In the blue tent my breathing
is smooth and easy, my sleep
restful and healing. Dreams
come, but never nightmares,
not like those I suffer in bed,
where I shake and cry out
for someone to help me,
someone who never comes.
In the tent, I close my eyes.
Before falling asleep, I think
about the moon and its light.
The moon spends the night
with me, and we journey

from east to west together.
An hour before the sun rises,
I emerge from my tent and stand
in the yard by my dark house
while the blue mists of dawn
wash the past and future clean.

The Secret

The first cold day of the year
I put on an old coat.
In the left front pocket—
a smooth black stone.

I haven't worn this coat in years,
though for a decade
it was the trusty coat I wore
on all my journeys,

journeys I'd mark with stones
carried home and arranged on shelves
to hold (as only stones can) memories
of the secret places I'd known.

But this black stone in my coat—
where did it come from?

The White Road

Just a man at a desk, writing—
lamplight on his hands,
the pen and the paper,
the endless white road of the poem.

Lamplight on his hands,
he writes about someplace far away,
the endless white road of the poem
a path to high country and still waters.

He writes about someplace far away—
meadows, wildflowers, crags, and clouds.
A path to high country and still waters,
this poem he will follow to the end.

Meadows, wildflowers, crags, and clouds—
more real than night or the coming dawn.
This poem he will follow to the end.
He will persist until he is nothing.

More real than night or the coming dawn—
the pen and the paper.
He will persist until he is nothing—
just a man at a desk, writing.

Oil for My Lamp

Like everyone else in town,
I fell victim to the epidemic
of loneliness. But when I saw
people setting their own homes
on fire, I loaded my old mule
and walked up the mountain.
With a hatchet I cut saplings
and built a dry and sturdy hut.
In the forest and sunny glades,
I gathered herbs and mushrooms,
dug chicory root from hard dirt
with the knife I always carry.
I tended a cooking fire of twigs,
boiled rainwater in an iron pot,
sat on a mat and wrote poems
onto river rocks, like Han Shan.
Nights of the harvest moon,
I wandered hillside orchards,
stealing apples from the rich.
I've heard the rich are never
lonely—they have shadows
for companions, and servants
who whisper tales of love
in exchange for a bowl of rice.
But I don't believe in rumors
or idle stories. I believe only
in the wind, and that it is good
to keep a store of oil for my lamp.

The Proposal

Because I find you beautiful
and see in you a kindred spirit,
I bend my knee and propose.
Come with me. Leave everything
now. My mule is out back, waiting.
It's not only blind, but also lame—
a stalwart companion nonetheless,
and loyal, and I don't have the heart
to put it down. Perhaps we can walk
beside it. I think you will find life
romantic, dark nights in the woods
by a small fire. I can skin a rabbit,
and as long as you don't mind
eating rabbit for the rest of your life,
we'll be happy. It's late November,
so we'd better start moving south
before the snows come in earnest.
If we don't make it, perhaps we may
find an abandoned house or barn.
We'll hold each other to keep warm
before we finally freeze to death.
Our love will be so great, the living
who find us will have to break our bones
to pry and crack and tear the two of us apart.

Downsizing

When the time finally comes,
as we know it assuredly will,
what will happen to my books?
I picture all my Rilke volumes
carried in a box out the door.
There goes Galway Kinnell.
There goes Adrienne Rich.
Farewell, sweet Anne Sexton.
Perhaps we'll meet in heaven.
For now, let me hold them
one last time in my hands
and listen to what they say.
Let me place them on the table,
their handsome covers in the sun,
and just enjoy our time together.
Soon all the clocks will wind down.
What to do when there is no book,
only empty mind and the high
clouds of poetry blowing away?

Blue

September 28, 1991

The night Miles Davis died
he came to me in a dream.
I was in Paris, delirious with fever,
and had no idea what day it was
or whether I'd live to see tomorrow.
Miles climbed the winding stairs
to the hotel's third floor, came in
and sat on the edge of my bed,
took my hand in his soft hand,
and invited me to join his band
in heaven. "On what instrument?"
I asked, turning on my pillow.
Miles said, "Richard, it's heaven.
Play any instrument you please."
"The marimba," I said. I told him
I'd always loved the rosewood bars,
the music of the mystical resonators.
Then my fever spiked. I swooned
in a dizzy mix of dread and euphoria.
Miles whispered, "Cool, man, cool."
Then he told me it's true: in paradise
all our tears are wiped away forever,
but that maybe a marimba in heaven
would help us remember what it was
to weep so much and so fiercely in life.

Light Graces My Head with a Halo

This morning I rose slowly from bed
and drifted downstairs to the breakfast table.

By the tall window that is ever luminous,
refracted light had melted the cold butter,

making easy work for the knife's blade.
Then for one fugitive instant, I lifted

a freshly cut, thick slice of fragrant rye
and leaned in my chair, tilting the earth

one degree closer to the scorching sun
to toast the bread to perfect crispness.

Mercury

Mercury used in the process of hat making
caused many to go crazy.
  —The Complete Annotated History
    of Hats and Hat Making

Consider making hats—
cutting and shaping something that will fit
the average human head:
berets, soft and bohemian,
and sturdy workers' caps—
so much like making a poem.
A top hat of beaver fur takes time,
slowly steaming the hat into shape,
then trimming and lining, detailing.
Hat making echoes our devotion to a single line,
how poetry demands the mercury of love
that can drive a poet mad,
like the hatters of old at their scarred worktables,
shaking from the vapors and visions.

Walking Meditation

Normally I do a walking meditation
in my own yard, making the rounds
in summer on a ritual path that weaves
between sunlit boxwood sentinels
and a small, well-tended rock garden.
How easy it is—the sound
of birdsong in the air, a fleet
of high clouds on a sea of blue—
to think of nothing. But once,
during a troubled, austere autumn,
my mind brooded and became
unruly. I found myself in a ryokan
in the remote mountains of Izu, Japan.
A ryokan is a traditional country inn,
like the inn where Kawabata lodged
and wrote his novel *Snow Country*.
I was a mere tourist, but my retreat
had ponds with carp, a red footbridge.
I slept on a tatami mat behind a shoji.
I bathed in the hot springs. I ate well
at a low table, served by a kneeling girl
whose laughter and kindness healed me.
At night I was given a painted kimono
and walked through a bamboo forest,
moonlight touching the towering trees,
paving stones under my wooden sandals.
I stepped slowly, respectfully, quietly.
My mind was the wind moving
through the bamboo's green columns.
I heard the dark counting its blessings
and branches saying prayers of gratitude.

Folly

In eighth grade, whenever I visited my sweetheart,
I'd cross the wide bridge over the Lafayette River
and ride my bike down Norfolk's narrow streets
past a garden with an arbor-temple of wisteria
that sheltered a ten-foot-tall bronze Buddha.
It would be years before I knew to call it a folly,
an absurd piece of garden architecture, a madness
meant solely for delight. In all my hometown,
where coal dust rose from the coal piers and fell
like black snow on our houses, there was nothing
like that garden with the smiling, seated Buddha.
The folly always lightened my spirits as I rode past,
and whatever despair or hope had troubled me
would lift as I pedaled—fast as I could pedal—
        toward Lilly's house.

Climbing

My daughter is a naturally gifted painter.
When we couldn't find a palette knife,
she painted with a silver garden trowel.
As she painted, she told me her truest gift
is her ability to climb, that she knows trees
and how to get up their trunks, how to use
her arms and legs to pull and push from
one branch to the next. "To get to the top?"
I asked. "No," she said. "Just climbing—
climbing for its own sake and nothing else."

House

On the coldest day of winter,
I shut off the furnace.
It's early morning, icy; I'm alone
in the chilled house and glad.
Soon the room is cold enough
that, sitting at my writing desk,
I can see breath clouds when
I blow on my hands to warm them.
I go upstairs and pile every blanket
in heavy layers on the big bed.
I crawl in and pull the covers
over my head. I want to stay here
until spring comes, when I shall rise
and go out looking for something
to eat. But that's not how it happens.
My wife and daughter come home
and shake me, telling me the house
is freezing, and asking if I'm crazy.

Astronomy

The white-haired astronomer is walking
across the quad with his colleague, talking
about the universe, the unseen order of things
swirling to the farthest reaches of the cosmos.
His young colleague, a nuclear physicist,
recognizes the subatomic constituency of reality
and sees in the smallest neutron the truth
of his friend's rhapsodies. They walk along—
talking, gesticulating, excited. People in love
should be so excited, eyes bright, full of genius
and madness, knowing they are on the right path,
they can feel it, they believe it, and more importantly,
they can prove it on a blackboard with a piece of chalk.

The Earth

Whenever I stand on some height—
a roof's edge or a balcony far above the street—
I think about jumping.

Beneath the endless dome of the sky—
I can't not picture it—
the body twirling in space as it drops.

I look down from a tower or rampart,
and the thought alone makes my knees go weak
and fills my head with vertigo.

And yet I can't help myself.
On a cliff's crumbling ledge, I'll lean forward
until I lose my balance and start to fall.

Then the windmills of my arms
wing me backward
until I regain my footing on the earth,

which is neither round nor spinning—
I tell my pounding heart—
but flat and perfectly safe for me to stand on.

Snakes

It's been a lifetime
since I've seen a snake
slither across the lawn
or scribble the letter *S*
on a sandy riverbank
or coil on a rock to sleep.

Decades ago in Georgia,
it was nothing
to see a snake every day
on the lawn or by the shed,
though snakes never failed to startle,
appearing from nowhere.

Copperheads, rattlesnakes,
diamondbacks, gopher snakes—
I chanced upon them all underfoot.
And how they'd wake me!
The green world came to life
and all day my mind stayed on guard.

In summer,
I'd watch the black snake
wrap itself around the bent branch
above the picnic table,
slough off its skin,
and slowly slip down to the ground.

If I could, just once more
I'd like to hide in the swamp—
perfectly still, invisible—
and watch the fanged water moccasin
lift into a question mark
before striking a fat bullfrog.

I don't even remember my last snake.
Maybe it was the checkered garter snake
my neighbor's cat, Chester,
proudly brought to my screen door,
the prize writhing in its mouth,
then dropped on the front porch as a gift.

Contentment

I like the folding chairs from the past,
those light metal ones that opened
with colorfully crossed nylon straps
that frayed like a pair of old jeans.
The chairs had wooden armrests,
and that meant everything to me,
knowing there is nothing better
than resting one's tired arms.
I used to sit in those chairs and fish
the small lake behind my house,
thinking about nothing, not even
fish, what they might be doing
under the dark water. I savored
the sweetness of the moment,
the quietude, not the bobbing buoy
or the reeling in, or even the feasting
that would come after a good long day.
I most enjoyed those times when
I caught nothing, when I simply
watched the high clouds float over,
hiding the sun and sending a chill,
then unveiling it to shine on my face—
my face that held no expression,
as blank as a poem about contentment,
that feeling so difficult to put into words,
no poet has ever dared try, and maybe never will.

Sons

My grown sons live by codes of honor
and dwell in the light of this world
by letting go of everything but grace.
I can't help but wonder who they are
and where they come from. In summer,
their brief visits are often unexpected
as if they just dropped in from heaven.
They park their cars in the driveway
and find me in the lush backyard—
a bone-weary man digging his grave,
an unfinished wooden coffin resting
on a pair of worn sawhorses, their father
doing the old work that's never done.
I wear a blue bandanna tied over my head,
and as they stand on the deck and ask
how I'm doing, I lean on my tall shovel
and tell them I couldn't imagine doing
better if I tried. From a jug I take a long
drink of water, wipe sweat from my eyes,
and ask them to tell me about their lives,
what mischief they've been up to lately,
all the things they've been thinking,
leaving out no detail, knowing there is
nothing too terrible and nothing too
wonderful for a father to hear from his sons.

Communion with My 96-Year-Old Mother

Because it is difficult for my deaf mother to rise,
much less walk the aisle and kneel at the altar,
the acolytes served us Communion in the pew
at the Christmas Eve service at Saint Andrew's.

The young boy and young girl leaned toward us
as they offered the holy wafer and blood of the wine.
And though my mother is no longer able to speak,
she sat upright and clearly said, "Thanks be to God."

Later that night, we sat by the fire. Now when I talk
to my mother, I speak in the most literal manner,
my sentences clear and direct, usually intended to
narrate the passing moment—the fire turning to coals.

With her brilliant eyes my mother reads my lips
and senses in my every word a thousand thoughts.

Quixotic

In a silk-lined tweed suitcase
trimmed in black leather
and secured with straps and buckles,
I pack my necessaries:
a pearl-handled straight razor
and my father's tortoiseshell mirror,
a leather flask and onyx field glasses.
My wife reminds me not to forget a toothbrush,
my pills, some cash and cell phone,
even though she knows
all I require in Madagascar or Tibet
are a few starched shirts,
a greatcoat, straw hat, and tattered passport.
She knows I take only what I need—
a few thin books
and a box of linen stationery
with gold envelopes
so I can send home a few simple words to her.

Grace

The task of the poet is to provide poems
that will help people live, as city workers
sawing storm-downed trees into stove-length
chunks provide firewood we need to survive
another winter. For a winter will come when
we will have no fire, no home, a winter when
people will walk two or three long, cold miles
for a roof, a modest meal, a metal folding chair
on which to sleep. There will come a time we
will have to rely on men debating unwritten laws,
laws governing fortune and fate, where we live
or die. The senate will meet, the people will be
wandering from shelter to shelter, there will be
referendum after referendum. In those days
people will need poems of joy and happiness,
poems at least as useful as wildflowers—
corn poppy, cosmos, and feverfew picked
from summer roadsides and placed in halls
on long tables where widows and orphans
bow their heads to give thanks before eating.

Avalon

Yes, I know what is said
about the order of things,
that next comes the cane,
the walker and wheelchair,
then the cold grave's oblivion.
But I still love my wife,
my children. I enjoy each day
of life in the little house
my daughter calls Avalon,
full of surprises and delights,
like this bright moment
in the garden in the sun,
when a praying mantis
lands on my left forearm,
turns his head, and studies me.
The spiritual way he folds
his long green wings
makes me believe he's here
on a heavenly mission
and is actually saying a prayer.
After checking on me,
the mantis will return and report
that I gratefully received
every message, attended
to all heralds from beyond,
and did not wait for gates
to swing open, but long ago
stepped through to where it is always joyful.

About the Author

Richard Jones is the author of several books of poetry, including *Country of Air*, *The Blessing: New and Selected Poems*, *Apropos of Nothing*, *The Obscure Hours: Translations*, and *Stranger on Earth*. He is also the award-winning editor of *Poetry East* and over the last four decades has curated its many anthologies, such as *The Last Believer in Words*, *Bliss*, *Origins*, *Wider than the Sky*, and *London*. He lives north of Chicago with his family.